KEYS TO UNLOCKING YOUR INSTAGRAM POTENTIAL

KEYS
TO
UNLOCKING YOUR
INSTAGRAM
POTENTIAL

"ONCE YOU'VE UNLOCKED THE DOOR, YOU CAN BECOME ANYTHING YOU WANT TO BE"

BY

TIARA DIONNE

KEYS TO UNLOCKING YOUR
INSTAGRAM POTENTIAL
Tiara Dionne

First Edition, 2021

Therealtiaradionne, Mrs_tiaradionne

TABLE OF CONTENTS

INTRODUCTION

"When you depend on people to feed you, you give them the power to starve you."

-Anonymous

I'm giving you the keys right here. The keys to change your life. Now you have to ask yourself, why is it important for you to grow your business and become successful? What would that mean for you and your family? Why do you need this?

Maybe you need this because you are looking for a change, you are tired of living on paycheck to paycheck, you believe there is more to life than just working under someone else for someone else. Maybe you want to build generational wealth for yourself and family. You want the freedom of being able to enjoy your life without having to worry about bills or even you just know the amount of lives you can impact of only you can understand how Instagram really works; if you answered yes to any of those reasons, then you truly have been divinely connected to the right place at the right time.

I will be giving you a power-packed book that respects your time.

With this book, you take control of your ideas, brand, business, and goals. Now is the time, and e-commerce and social media platforms are booming; so should you.

It is time to get on the bandwagon; start leveraging, growing, and monetizing your Instagram platform. Let's get to it!

Before reading any further, proclaim this affirmation to yourself:

I WILL BE THE FIRST MILLIONAIRE IN MY FAMILY BECAUSE I HAVE THE RIGHT TOOLS AND KNOWLEDGE IN MY HANDS.

I WILL READ THIS BOOK AND UNLOCK MY FULL POTENTIAL AS AN INFLUENCER THAT KNOWS HOW TO LEVERAGE AND MONETIZE NOT ONLY INSTAGRAM BUT OTHER PLATFORMS.

TODAY, I AM MAKING A DECISION TO NO LONGER MAKE EXCUSES, BUT TO LEARN WHAT I NEED TO TO ELEVATE TO THE NEXT LEVEL IN MY LIFE, RELATIONSHIPS, AND BUSINESS GOALS. I WILL ELEVATE.

IF YOU SAID THOSE AFFIRMATIONS RIGHT THERE, Then, you are on your way. Say it every day for 30 days! I challenge you. Freedom is a mindset, and change begins when you do something different.

Are you ready?! It's time; let's dive in...

CHAPTER ONE

THE PROBLEM WITH OVERTHINKING

Often we struggle with getting simple tasks done because we do not create a plan that we can strategically execute. Every business must have a plan in place of how a business should operate. YOU NEED STRUCTURE! We should be able to know the plan, and then pass that plan down to someone else. That is organizational leadership. Maybe you have been struggling with your online business because you have no plan, and when you have no plan, it's hard to make the vision possible and get the results we are hoping to achieve.

You need a plan for your vision. In a business the goal is to operate and execute (supply and demand). As a business owner, if you needed to hire someone to be a part of your team. How are you going to tell them what to do, if you don't even know what you are doing yourself? They will be doing what they want to do vs. you telling them what they need to do. Are you the worker or the CEO? C'mon now! YOU NEED A FOUNDATION BUILT NOT JUST A ROOF.

Some of us do not really understand how simple that concept truly is. When we think of our business on IG we think about Instagram, this is not Instagram's business; IT is YOURS, so this is why we need to have a strategic plan because IG is just the middle man. Do not worry about their algorithm and their hashtags. When you deliver valuable content, know how to network, and you have a clear game plan, all that other stuff is null and void. We are using IG to take us to the next level. Focus on what is important. That is building your empire, not a pretty little social media account. It is bigger than that! Get yourself out that box!

I need you to tell yourself right now "It is possible for me to become a millionaire by online sales." See yourself beyond your imagination. Building empires and creating generational wealth is a mindset.

Now that you know you need a plan on how to execute, than it's time to move past, "not being sure what to post" "Stop worrying about what can go wrong, and get excited about what can go right".- Anonymous

You are not going to change anything with a negative or defeated mindset. It takes 3Cs to succeed in unlocking your potential, and that is:

Confidence – Commitment – Character

The only way to grow is by getting uncomfortable. You need to put yourself out there and just do it. Practice makes perfect. How will you get better if you do not put yourself in position to excel? People need to see the face of the brand. They need to hear your voice.

Stop letting your emotions get involved and every other fear that keeps you from becoming the best version of yourself, and just do it! Make a decision that you will create a game plan, and post valuable content every day. Now is not the time to be taking social media breaks and vacations. If you are really serious about leveraging your IG account to expand your empire, then you need to stop making your commitment an option. You've already got what it takes, and you need to believe that, otherwise, you will never unlock your potential Period.

Ok. Let's Breathe and move on to the next.

Now that you have your confidence restored and your mindset ready to receive, it's time for phase two.

But wait! Let me make sure you retained what you just read.

Check-in:
What do you need in place for your business in order for your vision to be fulfilled? (Hint: Starts with a P)

What are the 3 C's you need in life to succeed?

"Stop worrying about what can go wrong, and get excited about what can go ___________".- Anonymous

Ok let's work. First things First. Get a Niche
Figure out your target audience. Who do you want to speak to? What do they need? How are you solving these groups' issues? What solution are you providing with the product or service you are offering?

The more specific we are, the more universal something can become. Life is in the details. If you generalize, it doesn't resonate. You need to know the exact group of people who need what you have. When you know your target audience, it is easier to understand their wants, needs, issues, what they do, where they go, and what they surround themselves with. You need to speak to your audience as though you know their exact struggles, thoughts, and the questions they would ask.

Key Homework:

You need to understand the foundation of your business. If you do not know what it takes to build the bottom, then you will never be able to get to the top. You cannot build a roof without the walls, stop trying to skip steps and understand this game brick by brick.

After figuring out your niche, come up with 1 or 2 services/ products that you are passionate about. Ask yourself, what problem do they solve? How will your products help your target audience?

What is your niche?

....

....

....

....

....

Who is your audience?

....

....

....

....

What is the problem that your audience has?

....

....

....

....

What is your product/service? (It should be in response to your target audience's problem)

....

....

....

....

What does your product/ service solve for your target audience?

....

....

....

....

Next step: Check your circle

As an individual that is trying to BECOME a millionaire, billionaire, building a empire and generational wealth, YOU MUST be around like-minded people. Surround yourself with people in your niche that are doing well. Immerse yourself in new knowledge and keep your energy high and ready to receive. When you are growing you cannot be conformed to a box and what you were used to doing. One of the main reasons we struggle with growth is because we become complacent and comfortable with what we are used to. The goal daily should be to learn a new skill, do, something different, and get work done every day.

Surround yourself with like-minded individuals who have similar goals they want to achieve. Now is not the time to be surrounding yourself with family/friends who are half stepping, asking you questions, not doing the work themselves, creating negativity vibes, distracting, draining you or throwing you off course. It's time to focus.

Find out who your influencers are. Who is an influencer? This is a person who is doing well in his/her niche, and by doing well, they are like-minded, similar goals in mind, they are passing down knowledge, they have a asset obtaining mindset, their audience is engaged, and it is clear they are making sales, they are passionate, they are real, and they have the "It" factor.

Research them, study them, learn from them, and apply what you've learned to your blueprint strategy.

Spilling the tea on who my influencers are:

@keziamw
@realtalkkim
@sleepisforsuckers
@wall_street_trapper
@19_keys
@thestudentloandoctor
@neodaviso
@tshirtmillionaires
@mgthemortgagesurgeon
@koeryelle
@thecrystalperkins

Research your influencers, study them, learn from them, and apply all you've learned to create your perfect blueprint strategy.

To-Do Activity

1. Write down three of your top influencers.
2. Study their conversations, learn their strategy, pay attention to their story (how they got where they are), figure out what's important, gather the questions their audience asks. Position yourself always to use them to get inspiration and motivation, and if it's an option, see if they can mentor you or join their anonymous groups.

CHAPTER TWO

THE BLUEPRINT: TAKE THE KEYS

"If the path be beautiful, let's not ask where it leads."
-Anatole France

This is how you run your business. After expelling all negative mindsets and creating a niche for yourself, the next thing is to know the Dos and the Don'ts.

First of all, you must ask yourself, why are you posting? And why do you choose a particular time to post? Posting just to post is useless. There has to be a strategy in place. You must learn to be intentional from this point about everything that you do, that is what the plan is in place to help you with strategy.

The Blueprint - The vision, the map, the layout of what you are looking to achieve. If you are trying to make sales. Every post should have a call to action.

Your post should do two things every time; bring knowledge and help. What are you providing to your audience when you post. Why are you providing it to them? Always ask yourself those questions. Stick to your niche, and try not to be all over the place the success is in your repetitive pattern.

Here is the relational selling formula 80% value, 20% ads. Always offer value. What does your current feed look like? Is it full of ads, everything you are selling? Or are you balancing it out between values, knowledge, product, inspiration?

Post other things; think of your feed like a TV show. Share your story, make it intriguing, and then allow your products to come in and be the commercial, but always try to get back to the show. They want to know your story, they want to know how you made it out, because that is where the relatable factor comes about. Share why you got started, why you came up with a solution for your products, spend time allowing the audience to get to know you. When people fall in love with you, they will easily fall in love with what you are selling. You are the product. Be transparent and authentic, and you will be in a position for fulfilling the know, like, and trust factor of your potential.

When you get to this place of finally being able to be you, you will be unstoppable! As you develop and become more confident, I encourage you to continue to feed yourself with knowledge that will elevate you. Keep retraining your mind. Visit the list of your influencers. Continue to say your positive affirmations daily. These are important for maintaining success habits. We must

BE CONFIDENT PUT YOURSELF OUT THERE! , COMMIT DAILY, and continue to build CHARACTER

(LEAVE THEM EMOTIONS SOMEWHERE ELSE).

HOMEWORK:
Revisit your influencer pages from time to time. Write down one thing you learned from them that you can apply to your life or business today?

RECAP:
Three Must-Haves for your Blueprint Strategy Post must:

1. Empowerment/ Inspire
2. Help
3. Provide knowledge

Here are a few tips:
Always ask yourself what solution does your product or service solve. When you remind yourself of that foundational question, then you can always use that as content and questions for your audience.

Share your story. Make your post/caption resonate with your audience. Create a post that can allow you and your audience to socialize. Be social. Share your story 80% of the time. Let the other 20% be about your product.

The Presentation of your business: Your Bio should be a strong statement that address (WHO you are,

WHAT you do, AND how your products/services help someone). It should be an elevator pitch.

Your page is literally like an online magazine. It shouldn't be messy. It should be pleasing to the eyes. Your picture posts must be clear and clean & not full of filters, poor lighting, and blurry backgrounds. Apps like **Canva** help make beautiful carousels to brand your products with.

CHAPTER THREE

THE TIME IS NOW: USE YOUR KEYS

"Every day in every way, I'm getting better."
-Emile Coue

"Every day in every way, I'm getting busier."
-Robert Cialdini

This is it; you are not here by accident. You are reading this because you've decided to take control of your life. You want to be the change you see, and I applaud you for taking this huge step. If you are reading this, you are another step closer to fully unlocking your potential. It's one thing to get the knowledge, but it's another to apply what you've learned. Right?

You have to realize that to get better is to get busier. Rise from your slumber and do the work needed. You have to make a decision to commit. It can't be, I'll do it today, and get back to it three days from now. Your work ethic has to be. "I will work every day. This is your business!

I often see people say on their business account "closed" or "taking a break" or even have private accounts LAWD! Consider this like any regular job, you need to either have someone come to fill in your spot or you just cannot take days off. I know It might be hard at first, but I promise it'll be worth it. Change your strategy, and you will change the game. You can't keep doing the same things and expect different results.

Implement all that has been addressed, effect changes, and your future self will thank you. Six months from now, you can be in a completely different space, mentally, spiritually and financially. Keep working and believing in yourself. You are either making mistakes or making money; on what side do you want to be?. I urge you to join the winning team, and with this book in your hands, you are one step away from unlocking potential sales.

I want the rules to be as effective as possible. But this will only happen to the degree that its fitness for duty is excellent. The truth is that we naturally will use it less and will be less able to cope efficiently with the decisional burdens of our day. But, we cannot allow that without a fight. The stakes have gotten too high. We need to act now.

Here are some extra keys:

1. Instagram stories should always be running. Use every other feature they have. If you aren't well acquainted with this, join me in my coaching and social media growth program (Link is in my Instagram bio).

2. Have a clear and clean bio of whom you are, what you do, and how you can help affect value.

3. Extra income: Charge people $5 to promote their business on your page. Figure out what people struggle with and come up with solutions. Become the expert.

4. Get involved. BE SOCIAL. BUILD A COMMUNITY.

5. Commit to posting daily, stick to your plan. It will draw your target audience closer to you and get people involved so long it's offering value. It is time to build those relationships.

What have you learned so far?

1. To make money, steps have to be taken. It goes from thinking about yourself, and what value you can offer to building relationships with your target audience to running ads to doing giveaways. This will grow your account for exposure. More exposure=more growth.

2. Find more ways to make money. Get creative. Memes add to the spice. Infuse them!

3. Be Brand representatives, promote with other big brands.

4. Help other people promote their business on your page. Collaborate with others of the same niche. You are not an island; you need people.

5. Invest in yourself. The more you invest in yourself, the better chance you have at improving and going on to the next level. Buy courses, buy study guides, attend Webinars, etc.

6. Once you get in the swing of things and you commit every day, put yourself out there. Go Live, post more videos of yourself. Share your story.

7. Get in deep- Connect with your audience. Let your story be the voice that guides you. Your audience needs to connect with the real you, so be open and vulnerable.

8. Always have a call to action on your caption or hashtags. ALWAYS.

Lastly, don't be afraid to say what you want to say to them. If you need to say "I offer several services, but one of them is 1 on 1 LIVE zoom call coaching. DM me if you are interested in learning more. Click on my bio if you want to purchase it" then say that!

This is where relationships happen, and you build real converting clients. Follow up with your clients. Get out there and see what your audience needs. Get involved in their lives.

Make friends. Build a strong community. IT IS SOCIAL MEDIA, GET SOCIAL.

While I cannot share everything in this book, the goal is to spur you on to action, get you off the ground, and in a position to leverage IG and make money. You have what it takes. The journey of a thousand miles begins with a step. Start yours today.

Thank you again for taking the time to read my e-book. You now have the keys to unlocking your potential and taking your IG to the next level. I want you to not be shy, reach out to me after you have read it, and share how it has transformed your life. I need your feedback. I actually offer several services, and one of them is 1 on 1 LIVE zoom call coaching. DM me the words @ mrs_tiaradionne "eBook" write me a review, and I will give you 50% off any of the next services you want to book with me.

I want you to know, I am rooting for you. My prayer is that you get to work. I know I gave you so much keys, but now is the time to apply what you learned, and if you already took my 7 day challenge. I am happy that you refreshed your knowledge. I hope you stay connected with me, and never stop working towards your goals and dreams. I believe in you.

xoxo, Tiara Dionne

"I see you, I love you, & you, & YOU are not alone"
☺ ☺ YOU GOT THIS!

www.ingramcontent.com/pod-product-compliance
Ingram Content Group UK Ltd.
Pitfield, Milton Keynes, MK11 3LW, UK
UKHW021933190726
13853UKWH00004B/1426